Transforming Into a Powerful Third, Fourth, or Fifth Grade Navigator of School Success

By Todd Jason Feltman, PhD

DEDICATION

In memory of my super stepfather, mentor, and friend, Alain du Pain. You are dearly missed! Your gusto and advice have encouraged me to write this handbook. Your conscientious work ethic and attention to detail has positively impacted my profession and education. I love you.

In memory of my four incredible grandparents and one amazing uncle who will always be remembered.

In honor of my mom, dad, stepmom, and brother, who will always be my wonderful heroes.

In honor of my teachers, assistant principals, principals, and professors who made a significant impact in my life.

In honor of my former and future fantastic third, fourth, and fifth grade Powerful Navigators of School Success.

PRAISE FOR THIS BOOK

Transforming Into a Powerful Third, Fourth, or Fifth Grade Navigator of School Success is easy to understand and full of helpful tips for anyone. I am confident this will not only guide young people through some of the most important academic years of their life, but it will implement strong habits that will be necessary for future success.

Elijah Lee, Youth Activist and High School Sophomore

This is a practical guide for students to help them navigate their own school experience. Todd's simple, powerful strategies will help them build the habits that can set them up for life-long success in the classroom and beyond.

Petal Modeste, Host, Parenting for the Future Podcast

Todd Feltman has written a fine book that provides excellent practical advice for primary school students. His focus on success is commendable. While many try to provide blueprints for being a successful student, Todd accomplishes it here. Teachers will also find this book an important resource. Read *Transforming Into a Powerful Third, Fourth, or Fifth Grade Navigator of School Success*, and learn!

Anthony G. Picciano, Professor, Instructional Leadership, School of Education, Hunter College and CUNY Graduate Center

I found *Transforming Into a Powerful Third, Fourth, or Fifth Grade Navigator of School Success* to be quite useful. One of the things that really stood out for me is that it is written by a practitioner...a teacher and a past administrator. The strategies in this book are sound, vast, and implementable. I recommend this book with zero hesitation nor reservation.

Principal Baruti Kafele, Education Consultant, Author, Retired Principal

Transforming Into a Powerful Third, Fourth, or Fifth Grade Navigator of School Success is a practical guide that teachers, children, and their parents will find helpful and insightful. Dr. Feltman's approach is accessible and written in a manner that children will appreciate. I wholeheartedly endorse this book!

Pedro Noguera, Dean, Rossier School of Education, University of Southern California

This is a power-packed book full of positivity. During these challenging times, we need books that inspire our children to be positive and give them ways to maintain a healthy mindset. This book is what we need at this time and place.

Luis E. Torres President of the NYC Elementary Principals Association

As an elementary school educator for over 16 years, I find this book to be a wonderful addition to every teacher's toolbox. It is creatively written to empower students to take ownership of their education. Dr. Feltman truly understands the mindset and needs of elementary school children. He created a resource for students that is interactive, reflective and written in child friendly language, making it fun and easy for students to comprehend.

Jaime Barron, Upper Elementary School Educator, New York City Public Schools

Dr. Todd Feltman's 100 universally applicable strategies for upper elementary students provide a blueprint for achieving "small wins" both inside and outside of the classroom. By encouraging students to practice only three to five strategies each week, they learn to set attainable goals, hold themselves accountable and reflect on who they are as both learners and children. Deploying Dr. Todd's strategies can make any student more confident and engaged.

Molly Danko, 2nd Grade Teacher and Former Hunter College Childhood Education Graduate Student

Transforming Into a Powerful Third, Fourth, or Fifth Grade Navigator of School Success is a wonderful and helpful interactive tool for students, their educators, and families. Students can advocate for themselves by having many useful strategies to choose from so that they can apply what works best for their learning style(s). The handbook is a great way for students to take the lead in their educational journeys. I wish this handbook existed when I was a student, but as a teacher I plan on encouraging my students to utilize it!

Betty Gerassi, Upper Elementary School Educator, New York City Public Schools.

Dr. Todd Feltman has written a practical, engaging guide for success in elementary school! His easy to follow steps, student-friendly language, and engaging characters will support third, fourth, and fifth grade students as they navigate and overcome the challenges they face. This guide empowers students to take control of their learning and, most importantly, to be in a constant state of self-reflection. Bravo, Dr. Feltman!

Jannell Jones-Stewart, Literacy Coach, Grades 3 to 8, New York City Public Schools and her son, Noah, 5th Grader

Who said that being a student would be easy? *Transforming Into a Powerful Third, Fourth, or Fifth Grade Navigator of School Success* helps students to unlock their fullest potential. Todd Feltman has written a clever book that offers valuable life lessons for all students. Stock up on this book and be assured to have a thriving classroom.

Cristina Cerezo, Elementary School Counselor, Third to Fifth Grade, New York City Public Schools

Dr. Feltman's *Transforming Into a Powerful Third, Fourth, or Fifth Grade Navigator of School Success* reminds students of the simple, daily things we do. These are things students may not realize impact their daily lives, positively or negatively. I like that students are asked to think about how they learn best. Knowing their own learning style can help students adjust and improve how they learn. Completing the reflection worksheets and taking notes also are great ways to help students remember. I would highly recommend this book to all third, fourth, and fifth graders.

Kristeine Flynn, Elementary School Counselor, Kindergarten to Fifth Grade, New York City Public Schools

Successfully navigating the school year can seem daunting to anyone. Todd Feltman's handbook is an essential tool for upper elementary school students and their parents. Feltman's insights and positive suggestions give students and parents a toolkit of straightforward practices and common-sense strategies that can be reviewed, on a regular basis, throughout the school year.

The guide's clear language will allow older elementary school students to gain confidence as they put the handbook's techniques into action. Parents of younger children can gently guide them to success. With these simple and straightforward methods students will be on the road to navigating a successful school year. And applying these strategies in elementary school will create a strong foundation for ongoing success in middle school and beyond.

Joanna Delson, Former High School English Teacher and Administrator

TABLE OF CONTENTS

FOREWORDS

I'm so happy you've decided to take charge of your education by reading this very practical handbook. If you don't take charge of your education, who will?!

By reading this book you're demonstrating that you want to be the best learner you can be. And it's so important that the author, Dr. Todd Feltman, lets you know that there are many different ways to learn and we each have our own unique way.

Dr. Feltman begins each chapter with "A Brief Powerful Story." Here's one I want to share with you as you begin this book... it may surprise you! When the author was your age -- yes, he once was, really -- I was his school principal. So, I was delighted when he asked me to write this brief foreword.

Here's what I believe is most important about this book: it's up to you to take active control of your learning! You can do it, I just know you can. Dr. Feltman did and now he's sharing these practical and helpful ideas with you. Read on and enjoy the adventures and challenges that await you as 3rd, 4th, and 5th graders.

Thanks for the honor of writing a foreword for this valuable and practical handbook, Todd.

Allan Shedlin
Former Principal, Midtown Ethical Culture School
Director & President, Daddying Film Festival & Forum (D3F)

I first met Dr. Todd Feltman when he asked me to speak to his class at Hunter College in New York City in December 2020. He wanted a student to be able to give advice and real-life lessons to future teachers. His evidence-based practices and trust in students immediately impressed me. Even from our first interaction, it became abundantly clear that Dr. Feltman was committed to finding new and innovative ways to prepare children to not only become strong students, but to become good people.

Dr. Feltman has served as a teacher in New York City Public Schools for 23 years, allowing him the time to gain vital experience and understanding of how to best work with a wide range of students. His work in education has extended beyond the classroom, serving as a city-wide literacy coach. Here, he served as an expert in his field, providing coaching to other professionals on how to provide students with the necessary resources to improve their reading and writing. He played a crucial role in the lives of many young teachers as they embark on a journey of educating and uplifting our future generations. Dr. Feltman has also served in the capacity of assistant principal, where he managed and provided leadership to an entire elementary school of passionate educators, staff, and students. It is an understatement to say that Dr. Todd Feltman is dedicated to his students and has knowledge and experience that could progress our modern education system.

Lucky for many of us, Dr. Feltman has decided to share his experience for students in grades three to five. His most recent book, *Transforming Into A Powerful Third, Fourth, or Fifth Grade Navigator of School Success Handbook*, is the perfect guide for any upper elementary school student preparing to move into a new and unknown era in their lives. This collection of tips and tricks provides amazing insight into how to move forward with being the best student you can be.

Now, this handbook is far from a basic piece of writing. It combines knowledge with realistic action steps for students. Within the handbook, a student will be able to learn a variety of strategies that will get any student ready for the day ahead, while increasing their confidence and self-esteem. They will not just read about the strategies, but they will have time to reflect on what they have learned as a student and learner. Studies show that both practices better equip young learners while allowing them to understand what works for them.

The lessons and amount of preparation this book provides can only be received through years of experience, and so I am so excited to be able to have this as a resource to refer others to. Dr. Feltman is a phenomenal educator, mentor, leader, and friend. His unconditional support and trustworthy words of encouragement have shown me that anything is possible. I am confident that by reading this book, any student will have the resources they need to make school work for them. In a time when students are struggling most, we as a community have an obligation to give young people the best shot. That is why I am proud to introduce Transforming *Into A Powerful Third, Fourth, or Fifth Grade Navigator of School Success Handbook.*

Elijah Lee
Youth Activist and High School Sophomore

INTRODUCTION

Salutations, Future Powerful Navigators of Success! I hope you are fully ready for this thrilling educational transformation! You can become a successful student and ultimately take charge of your education!

To get you started, read each of these questions twice. Using your juicy brains, think about your responses. You are also welcome to write down your answers. Happy thinking and responding!

- How would you feel to transform into a **Powerful Navigator of Upper Elementary School Success**?
- Are you aware that school does not come with a set of written instructions (like a board or video game) to help you navigate success?
- Are you in third, fourth, or fifth grade?
- Do you know how to be successful in school?
- Are you organized or disorganized?
- Are you able to stay focused during instruction or when your teacher(s) are speaking to you?
- Do you always finish or struggle to complete your homework on time?
- Do you follow classroom and school rules or agreements, or often get in trouble?
- Do you get along with your teacher(s) and classmates?
- Do you like or dislike school?
- How are you doing as a reader, writer, or mathematician?
- Do you know how to take charge of your education?

o Would you like one-hundred student-friendly practical strategies that could help you navigate school success?

Congratulations on beginning to read this handbook. I wish I had read this book when I was a third, fourth, or fifth grade student. It would have helped me navigate school success. I wrote this book because I wanted you to be prepared and successful.

Each chapter begins and ends with a short fictional narrative. Powerful Pencil and Successful Stapler, the two main characters, are best friends and classmates. They will also be your guides throughout the book. You are encouraged to color in the illustrations.

There are 100 strategies in this handbook. Don't worry, you don't have to memorize them. The strategies found within each of the six chapters are grouped by a common theme. This book starts with before school strategies and concludes with next school day preparation strategies. After each strategy, you will notice a brief explanation of the "Why" to support your curiosity. Helpful reminders and checklist items are included.

On every **strategy** page you can add an illustration and/or helpful notes if you choose to. At the end of each chapter, you will have an opportunity to reflect on the strategies you learned. Share these strategies with your classmates, friends, teachers, siblings, and family.

These strategies should help you become successful in school and throughout life. Hopefully, your grades will improve.

How can I effectively use this handbook?

1. Read through the entire handbook once.
2. Reread, underline, and highlight each chapter.
3. Draw and/or write notes for each strategy.
4. Practice three to five strategies each week.
5. Reread this handbook at any time to review strategies.

To begin your transformation into a Powerful Navigator of School Success, you should complete this brief student profile. Good luck and have fun on this strategic educational journey!

MY STUDENT PROFILE

I recommend that you share your completed profile with your teacher(s) and parent.

First Name _____

Gender _____

Age: _____

Grade: _____

Part One
My Learning Style

It is important to know how you learn best, which could help you achieve and be joyful in school and at home.

Directions:
- Select the two matching words shown in either line 1, 2, 3, or 4.
- Write the first matching word on the first blank line, and the second matching word on the second blank line.

Learning Styles
1. listening   auditory
2. speaking   verbal
3. seeing   visual
4. doing   kinesthetic

<u>Example</u>
<u>I choose line #3.</u>
I learn best by **seeing**, so therefore I am a **visual** learner.

I learn best by _____, so therefore I am a (n) _____ learner.

<u>Part Two</u>
Directions:
Please write your response for each sentence prompt on the line(s) provided.

My favorite book is _____.

My favorite subject is _____ because

_____.

My least favorite subject is _____

because _____.

In school, I am successful at _____.

At home, I am successful at _____.

In school, I struggle with _____.

For fun, I like to _____.

When I grow up I want to become _____ because

_____

Three ways to describe a great teacher are _____,

_____, and _____

One way to improve my classroom or school would be to

_____

CHAPTER 1

I CAN BE SUCCESSFULLY PREPARED TO BEGIN MY SCHOOL DAY

A BRIEF POWERFUL STORY

"Good morning, Future Powerful Navigators of School Success! I hope you slept well," says Powerful Pencil. The third grade students are quickly getting out of bed.

"We must do our before-school preparation! Are you ready?" whispers Powerful Pencil.

The children enthusiastically reply, "Yes!" They began doing their before school productive routines. Successful Stapler is doing yoga. After that, she will eat a hard boiled egg and a slice of whole wheat toast.

SNEAK PREVIEW OF STRATEGIES

 To prepare yourself, Powerful Pencil and Successful Stapler would like you to read and visualize each strategy.

Are any of these strategies part of your daily routine? If yes, you can underline or highlight that strategy.

1. Do at least fifteen minutes of stretching and exercising (jumping jacks, sit-ups, push-ups, and/or yoga, etc.) every morning.

2. Wash up or take a shower every morning before going to school.

3. Eat a healthy breakfast at home or school. A healthy breakfast could include cereal and milk, whole wheat bread, yogurt, fruit, eggs, and juice.

4. Avoid eating candy and drinking soda before and during the school day.

5. Drink at least one eight-ounce cup of water before the school day begins.

6. You should always carry at least **three sharpened pencils** in your bookbag or keep them in the back of your desk.

7. If you bring any money to school, keep it in your front pocket until you need it. If you have a wallet, you can use that.

8. It is better not to bring fidget spinners, toys, or electronics to school unless your teacher requests it. They can be a distraction to the classroom community.

9. If you are allowed to bring a cellular phone to school, make sure to keep it in a safe place (your pocket or perhaps your teacher can lock it up).

10. If you bring a cellular phone to school, make sure it is on silent or turned off.

11. Whenever possible, do your best to arrive at school at least five minutes early every day.

STRATEGY #1

Do at least fifteen minutes of stretching and exercising (jumping jacks, sit-ups, push-ups, and/or yoga, etc.) every morning.

Why: Stretching and exercises can wake up your body and brain and provide you energy for the day.

<u>My Illustration</u>

My Helpful Notes

STRATEGY #2

Wash up or take a shower every morning before going to school.

Why: Washing yourself or showering could wake you up. You might feel refreshed and clean for the school day ahead.

Helpful Reminder: Ask a family member for permission before taking a shower.

My Illustration

My Helpful Notes

_____

_____

_____

_____

_____

_____

_____

_____

_____

_____

_____

_____

_____

_____

STRATEGY #3

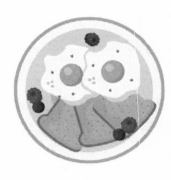

Eat a healthy breakfast at home or school. A healthy breakfast could include cereal and milk, whole wheat bread, yogurt, fruit, eggs, and juice.

Why: Your body needs healthy food to provide you with energy to learn.

<u>My Illustration</u>

My Helpful Notes

STRATEGY #4

Avoid eating candy and drinking soda before and during the school day.

Why: The sugar from the candy and/or soda may cause you to act silly and not be able to focus. You could get in trouble for misbehaving.

My Illustration

My Helpful Notes

STRATEGY #5

 Drink at least one eight-ounce cup of water before the school day begins.

Why: You do not want to be thirsty in the morning. Water hydrates your body and is necessary for your well-being. Not drinking enough water can cause you physical and mental health problems (http://consumer.healthday.com/kids-health-information-23/child-development-news-124/u-s-kids-not-drinking-enough-water-each-day-700291.html).

Helpful Reminder: Drink water during the school day, even if you are not thirsty.

My Illustration

My Helpful Notes

STRATEGY #6

 You should always carry at least **three sharpened pencils** in your bookbag or keep them in the back of your desk.

Why: You might never have to look for a pencil. You are taking charge of your education.

Helpful Reminders: Once you are finished using your pencil, put it in your bookbag or the back of your desk. Inform your teacher or parent if you don't have access to three pencils.

- Do you have **three sharpened pencils** in your bookbag or in the back of your desk?

My Illustration

My Helpful Notes

STRATEGY #7

If you bring any money to school, keep it in your front pocket until you need it. If you have a wallet, you can use that.

Why: Your money will be safer in your front pocket and/or a wallet. If you take any loose bills or coins out of your pocket, your money might get lost. You will avoid becoming frustrated over lost money.

Helpful Reminder: Whenever you wear sweatpants without a pocket zipper, you should keep your money in another safe spot.

My Illustration

My Helpful Notes

_____

_____

_____

_____

_____

_____

_____

_____

_____

_____

_____

_____

_____

_____

STRATEGY #8

It is better not to bring fidget spinners, toys, or electronics to school, unless your teacher requests it. They can be a distraction to the classroom community.

Why: The fidget spinners, toys and/or electronics could get lost, stolen, or taken away by the teacher. You need to be able to concentrate in your classroom and complete your work.

My Illustration

My Helpful Notes

STRATEGY #9

 If you are allowed to bring a cellular phone to school, make sure to keep it in a safe place (your pocket or perhaps your teacher can lock it up).

Why: You do not want to lose your cellular phone; therefore, you must take responsibility for your belongings. If you take it out during the school day without permission, your teacher will take it away from you.

<u>My Illustration</u>

My Helpful Notes

STRATEGY #10

 If you bring a cellular phone to school, make sure it is on silent or turned off.

Why: The ringing or vibration will distract you, the other students, and your teacher.

○ Did I remember to put my cellular phone on silent or turn it off?

<u>My Illustration</u>

My Helpful Notes

_____

_____

_____

_____

_____

_____

_____

_____

_____

_____

_____

_____

_____

_____

STRATEGY #11

Whenever possible, do your best to arrive at school at least five minutes early every day.

Why: You do not want to miss any new learning, nor do you want your grades to decrease. When you walk into class late, it is a disruption to the teacher and other students. Being on time is very important for your education and future job.

Helpful Reminders: If you are late to class, make sure to quietly apologize to the teacher. Whenever possible, you can politely ask your parent or family member to bring you to school at least five minutes early.

<u>My Illustration</u>

My Helpful Notes

A SHORT SUCCESSFUL STORY

As Powerful Pencil is walking to school, he sees his best friend, Successful Stapler, in the distance. He waves hello. In their classroom, Successful Stapler enthusiastically states "I have been practicing these before school strategies. I know that it will be a smoother day!" Powerful Pencil energetically gives her a thumbs up. He is glad that he exercised for fifteen minutes at home this morning.

In the next chapter, Powerful Pencil, Successful Stapler, and the other students can't wait to connect with their teachers.

Reflection Time

Powerful Pencil and Successful Stapler would like you to reflect on this chapter.

Which **two strategies from this chapter** would you like to immediately practice and **why?**

Strategy # _____
Page #   _____
Why: _____

_____

_____

_____

_____

_____

Strategy # _____
Page #   _____
Why: _____

_____

_____

_____

_____

_____

CHAPTER 2

I CAN SUCCESSFULLY DEVELOP POSITIVE RELATIONSHIPS WITH MY TEACHERS

A BRIEF POWERFUL STORY

At morning arrival in the schoolyard, Successful Stapler confidently says, "I hope my teachers get to know and like me. Otherwise, it will be a long school year!" Then, Powerful Pencil arrives holding a red Macintosh apple.

He energetically says that "Creating positive relationships with teachers is amazing!" The third grade students give high-fives to Powerful Pencil and Successful Stapler. The smile on their faces are priceless. The enthusiastic students are ready to read the strategies from this chapter.

They yell, "We can't wait to tell our teachers about our interests, hobbies, and dreams!"

SNEAK PREVIEW OF STRATEGIES

 To prepare yourself, Powerful Pencil and Successful Stapler would like you to read and visualize each strategy.

Are any of these strategies part of your daily routine? If yes, you can underline or highlight that strategy.

12. Say "Good morning, [teacher's name]," or "Good afternoon, [teacher's name]," when you first see your teacher(s) each morning and/or afternoon.

13. If your teacher(s) presents an exciting and enjoyable lesson, let him or her know that you enjoyed it.

14. Get to know the interests and hobbies of your teacher(s).

15. If you are having a bad day, inform your teacher(s) at the beginning of class.

16. If you don't like a particular teacher, you should never treat him or her in a rude manner. Work hard and be an active participant in the class.

17. If you are having a disagreement with your teacher, ask to speak privately with him or her after class.

18. Whenever you have a problem with another student at school, speak to your teacher first before you discuss it with your parent.

19. Wait for your teacher to dismiss you before packing up your bookbag or standing up to leave.

20. Avoid disrespecting a substitute teacher. What if you were a substitute teacher? How would you want to be treated?

21. You should only go to the nurse if you really need it. Asking to go to the nurse to avoid doing work or because you're tired, bored, frustrated, or grumpy is unacceptable.

STRATEGY #12

Say "Good morning, [teacher's name]," or "Good afternoon, [teacher's name]," when you first see your teacher(s) each morning and/or afternoon.

Why: You are showing your teacher(s) that you are friendly and respectful and that you appreciate him or her.

My Illustration

My Helpful Notes

STRATEGY #13

If your teacher(s) presents an exciting and enjoyable lesson, let him or her know that you enjoyed it.

Why: You could be proud of yourself for complimenting your teacher. You are reflecting about what you just learned. It might help your teacher with planning future lessons that will interest you.

My Illustration

My Helpful Notes

STRATEGY #14

Get to know the interests and hobbies of your teacher(s).

Why: You might feel more comfortable in his or her class and, therefore, like being with that teacher.

Helpful Reminder: You could also share your interests, hobbies, and dreams from your student profile with your teacher(s).

<u>My Illustration</u>

My Helpful Notes

STRATEGY #15

If you are having a bad day, inform your teacher(s) at the beginning of class.

Why: Your teacher(s) will be aware of your mood and can support you with having a better day.

Helpful Reminders: You can also tell the lunch/recess staff. Despite the type of day you are having, you are still expected to follow the classroom rules. If you're in a bad mood, you should not disrespect your teacher or the other students.

- o Did I tell my teacher(s) and lunch/recess staff that I was having a bad day?

My Illustration

My Helpful Notes

STRATEGY #16

If you don't like a particular teacher, you should never treat him or her in a rude manner. Work hard and be an active participant in the class.

Why: You are not going to like everybody you meet in this world; therefore, you need to figure out how to get along. Please remember that the goal of your teacher is to instruct you, not to make your life difficult.

Helpful Reminder: You can ask for help with this situation from another teacher, your assistant principal, or your parent.

My Illustration

My Helpful Notes

STRATEGY #17

If you are having a disagreement with your teacher, ask to speak privately with him or her after class.

Why: Privately discussing a disagreement can help solve the problem without creating distractions for the other students in your classroom.

Helpful Reminder: Calmly explain to your teacher what is upsetting you.

<u>My Illustration</u>

My Helpful Notes

_____

_____

_____

_____

_____

_____

_____

_____

_____

_____

_____

_____

_____

STRATEGY #18

Whenever you have a problem with another student at school, speak to your teacher first before you discuss it with your parent.

Why: Speaking to your teacher about it immediately provides you both with an opportunity to resolve the problem right away. Hopefully, it won't continue to bother you.

<u>My Illustration</u>

My Helpful Notes

STRATEGY #19

Wait for your teacher to dismiss you before packing up your bookbag or standing up to leave.

Why: You might miss a learning opportunity or an important reminder that will affect your grade. Additionally, it is a disruption to the teacher and other students.

Helpful Reminder: Your teacher is the one who dismisses the class—not you. It is inconsiderate to prepare to leave the classroom while your teacher is finishing the lesson.

My Illustration

My Helpful Notes

_____

_____

_____

_____

_____

_____

_____

_____

_____

_____

_____

_____

_____

_____

STRATEGY #20

Avoid disrespecting a substitute teacher. What if you were a substitute teacher? How would you want to be treated?

Why: If you choose to misbehave with a substitute teacher, you might get in trouble and be disappointed in yourself.

Helpful Reminders: Being a substitute teacher is one of the toughest jobs in education. If you don't behave well for the substitute teacher, you will upset your teacher.

My Illustration

My Helpful Notes

STRATEGY #21

You should only go to the nurse if you really need it. Asking to go to the nurse to avoid doing work or because you're tired, bored, frustrated, or grumpy is unacceptable.

Why: You will still have to do work and solve your problem. The nurse will not be able to do anything for you. School nurses are hired to take care of students who are injured or not feeling well.

Helpful Reminder: If you are tired, bored, frustrated, or grumpy about your schoolwork, or if you are just in a bad mood, speak to your teacher rather than ask to go to the nurse.

My Illustration

My Helpful Notes

A SHORT SUCCESSFUL STORY

"We like our teacher! She makes learning exciting!," yell the thoughtful third graders. They were gathered near the jungle gym during recess. Powerful Pencil and Successful Stapler both smile and give each other fist bumps. All morning, they both overhear genuine compliments from the other students about the excellent lessons being taught. Successful Stapler was clapping her hands together to recognize the joy. Rainbow-colored plastic staples magically appear on the ground as she claps.

Unfortunately, that morning, Powerful Pencil arrives at school in a bad mood. He didn't sleep well and had an argument before school with his younger brother, Possible Pencil.

As the students are sitting down for the morning meeting, he whispers to his teacher, Ms. Always Helpful, "I am having a bad day." She listens closely and now is aware. Powerful Pencil's day got better. Powerful Pencil and Successful Stapler are both excited to learn how to become a responsible and helpful class citizen.

Reflection Time

Powerful Pencil and Successful Stapler would like you to reflect on this chapter.

Which **two strategies from this chapter** would you like to immediately practice and **why?**

Strategy # _____
Page #   _____
Why: _____
_____
_____
_____
_____
_____

Strategy # _____
Page #   _____
Why: _____
_____
_____
_____
_____
_____

CHAPTER 3

I CAN SUCCESSFULLY BECOME A RESPONSIBLE AND HELPFUL CLASS CITIZEN

A BRIEF POWERFUL STORY

Powerful Pencil is sitting as best he could in his classroom chair. The focused fourth grade students are sitting on the rug. Powerful Pencil raises his eraser. Their teacher, Ms. Mostly Interesting, calls on him. He requests to stretch and his teacher agrees. After Powerful Pencil sits down, the students curiously ask the teacher, "How can we become responsible and helpful class citizens?"

She quickly responds by stating, "Great question! Let's read these strategies and discuss them after recess." The students were excited to read and transform into responsible and helpful class citizens.

Successful Stapler enthusiastically said, "Positive Citizenship transformation time soon!"

SNEAK PREVIEW OF STRATEGIES

 To prepare yourself, Powerful Pencil and Successful Stapler would like you to read and visualize each strategy.

Are any of these strategies part of your daily routine? If yes, you can underline or highlight that strategy.

22. You must follow the classroom rules or agreements even if you don't agree with them.

23. Raise your hand during a whole-class lesson and wait to be called on.

24. You should never talk without being called on during a whole-class lesson, while the teacher, or another student is speaking.

25. Sit up straight (yet comfortably) and avoid putting your head on the desk.

26. You must remain in your seat unless you receive permission to get out of your seat.

27. Keep all four legs of your chair, desk, and table on the ground.

28. Avoid joking around with your friends during instruction and independent work.

29. If a classmate is bothering you, tell him or her to stop specifically what he or she is doing. Make sure to use a strong voice when talking

to that classmate! If that classmate does not listen to your request, let the teacher know.

30. If you are about to get into a physical fight with another student, you can say something such as this: "Let's discuss this. I don't want to get in trouble or injured, and I don't think you do either."

31. Avoid telling secrets, including rumors about students or teachers.

32. Avoid passing notes in class.

33. Nobody should exclude another student from sitting next to him or her and/or from playing with him or her.

34. If another student looks different from you or other students, do not make fun of him or her.

35. Avoid teasing and laughing at somebody to make him or her feel embarrassed and angry.

36. As a bystander (one who is present, but not taking part in the problematic situation), if you witness any student(s) being verbally bullied, physically bullied, or cyberbullied, immediately report it to an adult. Explain in detail what happened to that student and where the bullying took place.

37. Avoid leaving the classroom without permission.

38. Do not leave garbage on the floor in your classroom.

STRATEGY #22

You must follow the classroom rules or agreements, even if you don't agree with them.

Why: If you don't follow the classroom rules or agreements, you could get in trouble, and your grades will decrease. Rules or agreements are in place to help all students learn and not become distracted.

Helpful Reminders: You can ask your teacher to explain the purpose of each rule or agreement. You can request to share an idea for a new classroom rule or agreement.

My Illustration

My Helpful Notes

STRATEGY #23

Raise your hand during a whole-class lesson and wait to be called on.

Why: You want to show your teacher that you want to speak. If you call out without permission, you are disturbing the teacher and other students.

Helpful Reminder: Whenever you have something you really want to ask or share, write it down so that you won't forget to ask it. You can ask your teacher if you can write down your question or share information in the back of a notebook.

My Illustration

My Helpful Notes

STRATEGY #24

 You should never talk without being called on during a whole-class lesson, while the teacher or another student is speaking.

Why: It is impolite and distracts the teacher and other students. Teachers must be able to teach without interruptions. Students can also learn from what their classmates say.

Helpful Reminder: If you are confused by what the teacher or another student said during a whole-class lesson, raise your hand for an explanation instead of asking a classmate sitting near you.

My Illustration

My Helpful Notes

STRATEGY #25

 Sit up straight (yet comfortably) and avoid putting your head on the desk.

Why: Sitting up straight helps you focus. You would miss explanations that are written down because you can't see them. Putting your head down on the desk during a lesson without permission is disrespectful.

Helpful Reminder: If you have a headache or don't feel well, let your teacher know.

My Illustration

My Helpful Notes

STRATEGY #26

 You must remain in your seat unless you receive permission to get out of your seat.

Why: Remaining in your seat will help you be focused and safe.

Helpful Reminder: If you prefer to stand up during instruction, you should privately speak to your teacher.

<u>My Illustration</u>

My Helpful Notes

STRATEGY #27

Keep all four legs of your chair, desk, and table on the ground.

Why: You might get injured if you and the chair, desk, or table fall. Having even one leg of the chair, desk, or table off the ground is unsafe and a disruption to the learning environment.

Helpful Reminders: Avoid leaning back in your chair to protect yourself. Request to stand up for a few minutes if you feel the need to stretch your legs.

<u>My Illustration</u>

My Helpful Notes

STRATEGY #28

 Avoid joking around with your friends during instruction and independent work.

Why: You will get in trouble, and your grades will decrease. It will be difficult for the teacher to teach and for you and your classmates to learn.

Helpful Reminder: More appropriate times to joke around with your friends include during brain breaks, lunch, recess, or activities you participate in after school.

My Illustration

My Helpful Notes

STRATEGY #29

If a classmate is bothering you, tell him or her to stop specifically what he or she is doing. Make sure to use a strong voice when talking to that classmate! If that classmate does not listen to your request, let the teacher know.

Why: You are standing up for yourself. You have a right to be respected. Telling the teacher is not tattling; it is a technique to resolve a problem after speaking with that particular classmate.

My Illustration

My Helpful Notes

STRATEGY #30

 If you are about to get into a physical fight with another student, you can say something such as this: "Let's discuss this. I don't want to get in trouble or injured, and I don't think you do either."

Why: You are standing up for yourself through speaking. Settling conflicts through speaking does not make you look weak. Resolving an argument or disagreement using words is the most responsible and peaceful way to settle it. You don't want to physically harm yourself or another student.

<u>My Illustration</u>

My Helpful Notes

STRATEGY #31

Avoid telling secrets, including rumors about students or teachers.

Why: It is best to avoid this practice as it is unfriendly and can make other students and their teacher(s) angry.

Helpful Reminder: Students and/or teachers might become nervous that the secret is about them.

My Illustration

My Helpful Notes

STRATEGY #32

Avoid passing notes in class.

Why: It is a distraction to instruction and learning. The note can hurt the feelings of a particular student, several students, or the teacher.

Helpful Reminder: If you are caught holding a note, the teacher might require that you read it out loud.

My Illustration

My Helpful Notes

STRATEGY #33

Nobody should exclude another student from sitting next to him or her and/or from playing with him or her.

Why: It could hurt the feelings of that student. You have an opportunity to make a new friend.

<u>My Illustration</u>

My Helpful Notes

STRATEGY #34

If another student looks different from you or other students, do not make fun of him or her.

Why: Teasing about a student's physical appearance is unfriendly. Please think about how you would feel if the teasing were happening to you.

My Illustration

My Helpful Notes

STRATEGY #35

Avoid teasing and laughing at somebody to make him or her feel embarrassed and angry.

Why: Teasing and laughing at another student is disrespectful and hurtful. These actions create conflict.

My Illustration

My Helpful Notes

STRATEGY #36

As a bystander (one who is present, but not taking part in the problematic situation), if you witness any student(s) being verbally bullied, physically bullied, or cyberbullied, immediately report it to an adult. Explain in detail what happened to that student and where the bullying took place.

Why: You might be proud of yourself because you are reporting bullying to protect students. As an upstander (one who speaks up or takes action when another person is being bullied), you are taking charge of the situation.

My Illustration

My Helpful Notes

STRATEGY #37

Avoid leaving the classroom without permission.

Why: You will not be trusted, and you could get in trouble. Your teacher is responsible for your safety. If you walk out of your classroom without telling your teacher, you are creating unnecessary stress and it could be dangerous.

Helpful Reminder: If you feel frustrated or grumpy and need a quick walk and/or water break, raise your hand to request it.

<u>My Illustration</u>

My Helpful Notes

STRATEGY #38

Do not leave garbage on the floor in your classroom.

Why: Your classroom could become messy, and it is not the custodian's job to clean up after your mess.

Helpful Reminder: Before you leave your classroom, check your area for any garbage on the floor. Throw out any garbage that belongs to you.

<u>My Illustration</u>

My Helpful Notes

A SHORT SUCCESSFUL STORY

Powerful Pencil and Successful Stapler were joyfully eating pizza in the cafeteria. For the second time, they witness two male students bullying another male student. They both call him a wimp and also push him. That boy begins to cry and tells the two bullies to leave him alone. Powerful Pencil walks over to both of them and firmly says, "Stop!" Successful Stapler walks over to the assistant principal and explains what happened. The assistant principal takes immediate action. Later that day, the three students from the bullying incident chose to participate in a positive collaborative conflict resolution.

In the classroom, Powerful Pencil and Successful Stapler do a "bullying" role play in front of the other fourth graders. The students loudly clap. As a result of the positive impact from the role play and repeated strategic practice the other students became upstanders, even the two bullies. A week later, the three boys become friends and create a student-led group to prevent bullying. Ms. Mostly Interesting volunteers to be the group mentor.

Powerful Pencil and Successful Stapler hold a banner that reads *How Can I Successfully and Happily Learn?* The fourth graders are eager to know and can't wait to read the next chapter.

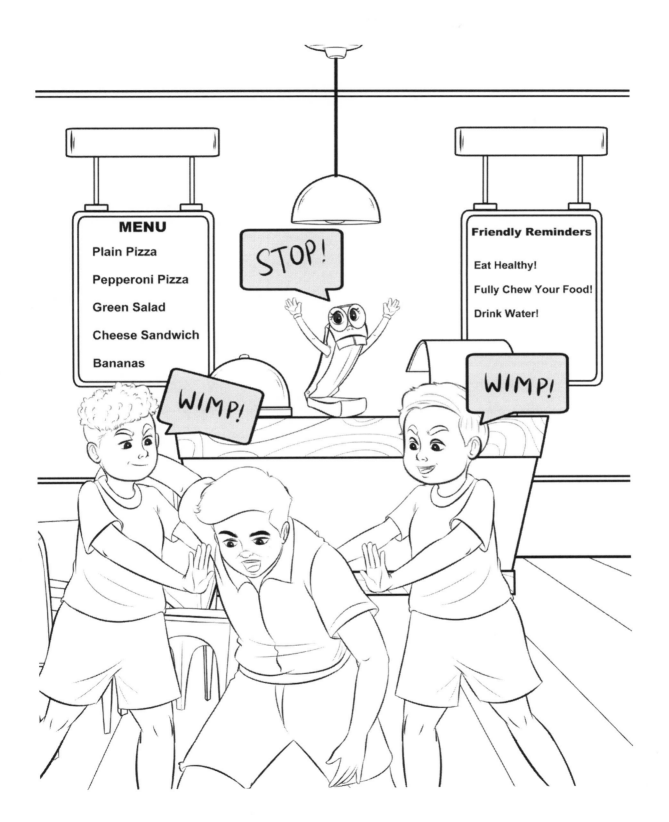

Reflection Time

Powerful Pencil and Successful Stapler would like you to reflect on this chapter.

Which **two strategies from this chapter** would you like to immediately practice and **why**?

Strategy # _____
Page #   _____
Why: _____
_____
_____
_____
_____
_____

Strategy # _____
Page #   _____
Why: _____
_____
_____
_____
_____
_____

CHAPTER 4

I CAN SUCCESSFULLY AND HAPPILY LEARN

A BRIEF POWERFUL STORY

The fourth grade students are jumping up and down in their classroom. They are eagerly cheering, "We want to be powerful learners! We can do it!" Meanwhile, Powerful Pencil was eating his apple in the hallway. He hears all of this excitement and walks quickly to the classroom. As soon as Powerful Pencil enters the classroom, he starts clapping and then taps his point. The children are smiling!

Powerful Pencil and Successful Stapler confidently says, "You all can definitely do it!" Ms. Mostly Interesting joyfully states, "It's time to read these multiple strategies. Happy reading!" The students begin enthusiastically independently reading the strategies.

SNEAK PREVIEW OF STRATEGIES

 To prepare yourself, Powerful Pencil and Successful Stapler would like you to read and visualize each strategy.

Are any of these strategies part of your daily routine? If yes, you can underline or highlight that strategy.

39. Write down every homework assignment and reminder in your same homework notebook or planner each day.

40. Before you leave your classroom, carefully review your homework notebook or planner to make sure you take home any handouts, books, notebooks, or folders that you will need.

41. Write down the phone number and/or e-mail address of a trusted friend in your class to contact whenever you are absent. You will be able to find out what was taught and the homework assignment on that day.

42. Ask your teacher to share helpful techniques on how to study for quizzes and tests.

43. Keep your classroom materials in your desk or seat sack, organized and neat.

44. Keep only the materials that you need on your desk or table.

45. Try to write neatly. It can be difficult. Just do your best!

46. Always write the date and topic on all your class notes, handouts, and work you complete.

47. Pay attention to your teacher.

48. Avoid daydreaming.

49. Use all the charts, posters, and word walls hung in your classroom to support you with learning.

50. Apply useful information learned in one subject to your other subjects.

51. If you don't know what a word means during instruction, ask your teacher.

52. Ask questions whenever you are curious or confused with any information. Don't be afraid to ask questions. It is likely that other students have the same question, but are not asking it.

53. Be an active participant, not a spectator, in the classroom. This means that you should be thinking, asking, and answering questions, and using what you learned to complete assignments.

54. Read the assignment or task description at least three times before you begin it.

55. If you are confused with an assignment or task's description or requirements, ask the teacher to explain them. Don't be embarrassed to request help.

56. During any group or partner task, take a leadership role or be an active participant.

57. Whenever you are asked to provide feedback on another student's work, make sure to always begin with a specific compliment. Suggestions should be shared in a friendly tone of voice, never rudely or sarcastically.

58. It is acceptable to disagree with a statement made by a teacher, student, or within a text. You must provide evidence to back up your disagreement. Whenever you disagree, respect in your tone of voice and body language is required. There should be no insults made toward the teacher or other students.

59. Ask your teacher how a lesson will help you in the real world.

60. Make connections to what you learn in school to your life outside of school.

61. Plan to eat lunch every day.

62. During outdoor recess, make sure to run around, be active, and have fun.

STRATEGY #39

Write down every homework assignment and reminder in the same homework notebook or planner each day.

Why: Using the same homework notebook or planner could help you with organization. Your homework grade might not decrease. You will be able to review reminders.

Helpful Reminders: Carefully copy down your homework. Double-check that you have correctly written everything down.

My Illustration

My Helpful Notes

STRATEGY #40

Before you leave your classroom, carefully review your homework notebook or planner to make sure you take home any handouts, books, notebooks, or folders that you will need.

Why: You do not want to receive a poor grade or get in trouble. Being unprepared for any of your classes is not acceptable.

Helpful Reminders: It is your responsibility to put the necessary homework materials in your bookbag. If you are a forgetful person, ask a classmate, friend, or your teacher to remind you of what you must take home.

<u>My Illustration</u>

My Helpful Notes

STRATEGY #41

Write down the phone number and/or e-mail address of a trusted friend in your class to contact whenever you are absent. You will be able to find out what was taught and the homework assignment on that day.

Why: You might not have to make up as much missed work. You will be acting responsibly and preparing for a future career.

My Illustration

My Helpful Notes

STRATEGY #42

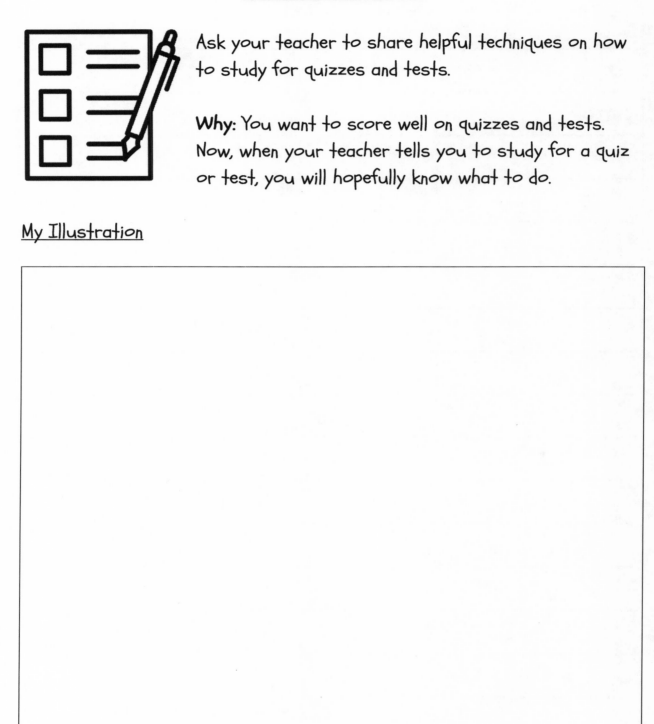

Ask your teacher to share helpful techniques on how to study for quizzes and tests.

Why: You want to score well on quizzes and tests. Now, when your teacher tells you to study for a quiz or test, you will hopefully know what to do.

<u>My Illustration</u>

My Helpful Notes

STRATEGY #43

Keep your classroom materials in your desk or seat sack, organized and neat.

Why: You want to be able to find your books, notebooks, folders, and supplies quickly. You do not want to waste any time searching for your classroom materials.

Helpful Reminder: You can put your notebooks, folders, and supplies on one side of your desk and textbooks, workbooks, and your independent reading book on the other side.

o Are my classroom materials neat and organized?

<u>My Illustration</u>

My Helpful Notes

STRATEGY #44

Keep only the materials that you need on your desk or table.

Why: You will be better able to pay attention and not become confused.

o Do I only have the materials I need for the current lesson on my desk or table?

My Illustration

My Helpful Notes

STRATEGY #45

Try to write neatly. It can be difficult. Just do your best!

Why: It will be easier for you, your teacher, and your classmates to read your work. Neat handwriting can help you with proofreading and studying.

Helpful Reminders: If you need help improving your manuscript handwriting or cursive writing, speak to your teacher or parent. You can ask your parent if they could purchase one of the recommended inexpensive handwriting practice books listed below.

Recommended Handwriting Practice Book Titles:
- *Printing Practice Handwriting Workbook, by Speedy Publishing LLC*
- *Handwriting Cursive Workbook, Grades 3 to 5, by Carson-Dellosa Publishing*

My Illustration

My Helpful Notes

STRATEGY #46

Always write the date and topic on all your class notes, handouts, and work you complete.

Why: When completing assignments and homework and studying for quizzes and tests, you could be organized and not waste time.

My Illustration

My Helpful Notes

_____

_____

_____

_____

_____

_____

_____

_____

_____

_____

_____

_____

_____

_____

STRATEGY #47

Pay attention to your teacher.

Why: This is your responsibility, and you do not want to get a poor grade. You could become smarter when you pay attention.

Helpful Reminder: As your teacher is instructing, you can focus your eyes on him or her.

<u>My Illustration</u>

My Helpful Notes

STRATEGY #48

Avoid daydreaming.

Why: You might miss important information and won't know how to complete your work.

Helpful Reminders: You could ask your teacher if you could sit in the front of the classroom. If you find yourself daydreaming, raise your hand and ask your teacher if you can stand up and stretch.

My Illustration

My Helpful Notes

STRATEGY #49

Use all the charts, posters, and word walls hung in your classroom to support you with learning.

Why: These supports can help you do better in every subject.

My Illustration

My Helpful Notes

STRATEGY #50

Apply useful information learned in one subject to your other subjects.

Why: Whenever you make a connection to another subject, learning can become enjoyable and meaningful.

<u>My Illustration</u>

My Helpful Notes

STRATEGY #51

If you don't know what a word means during instruction, ask your teacher.

Why: You will know what that word means, and learning can become more interesting.

<u>My Illustration</u>

My Helpful Notes

STRATEGY #52

Ask questions whenever you are curious or confused with any information. Don't be afraid to ask questions. It is likely that other students have the same question, but are not asking it.

Why: To achieve and be engaged, it is your responsibility to understand what you are learning. If the information is unclear, you must ask so you can know what is being taught.

My Illustration

My Helpful Notes

STRATEGY #53

Be an active participant, not a spectator, in the classroom. This means that you should be thinking, asking, and answering questions, and using what you learned to complete assignments.

Why: As an active participant, school could be exciting because you are taking charge of your learning. Being a student is your full-time job. You need to focus on doing your best.

My Illustration

My Helpful Notes

STRATEGY #54

Read the assignment or task description *at least three times* before you begin it.

Why: It is usually difficult to complete an assignment or task when you have read the description only once. Before you begin an assignment or task, it is important to understand what you need to do.

○ Did I read the assignment or task description *at least three times* before I began it?

<u>My Illustration</u>

My Helpful Notes

STRATEGY #55

If you are confused with an assignment or task's description or requirements, ask the teacher to explain them. Don't be embarrassed to request help.

Why: You want to correctly do an assignment or task to receive a good grade. If you don't understand an assignment, most likely there are other students in the class who don't either.

<u>My Illustration</u>

My Helpful Notes

STRATEGY #56

During any group or partner task, take a leadership role or be an active participant.

Why: You could find the task to be interesting when you actively participate. Since you are leading and/or actively participating, the task should be completed more quickly.

My Illustration

My Helpful Notes

STRATEGY #57

Whenever you are asked to provide feedback on another student's work, make sure to always begin with a specific compliment. Suggestions should be shared in a friendly tone of voice, never rudely or sarcastically.

Why: It is important for students and adults to first hear what they did well to build their self-confidence. Then, they are better able to listen to a suggestion and implement it.

<u>My Illustration</u>

My Helpful Notes

STRATEGY #58

It is acceptable to disagree with a statement made by a teacher, student, or a text. You must provide evidence to back up your disagreement. Whenever you disagree, respect in your tone of voice and body language is required. There should be no insults made toward the teacher or other students.

Why: Respectfully disagreeing supported by evidence is an essential skill that students need. If you learn how to properly disagree in school, it could support you throughout your life.

My Illustration

My Helpful Notes

STRATEGY #59

Ask your teacher how a lesson will help you in the real world.

 Why: If you understand how a lesson will help you outside of school, you may become more interested in a particular subject. School is preparation for your future career.

<u>My Illustration</u>

My Helpful Notes

STRATEGY #60

Make connections to what you learn in school to your life outside of school.

Why: Learning within and outside of school could become fascinating and useful.

<u>My Illustration</u>

My Helpful Notes

STRATEGY #61

Plan to eat lunch every day.

Why: You need energy to pay attention and do your best in your classes.

<u>My Illustration</u>

My Helpful Notes

STRATEGY #62

During outdoor recess, make sure to run around, be active, and have fun.

Why: Recess is a break for you to recharge your brain and body for the rest of the day. Physical exercise helps you relieve stress and can energize you to complete the remainder of the school day.

<u>My Illustration</u>

My Helpful Notes

A SHORT SUCCESSFUL STORY

At the beginning of the writing lesson, Successful Stapler has her notebook, folder, pencil, and eraser on her desk. Ms. Mostly Interesting walks by and states, "You're ready with those materials."

Powerful Pencil listens to the explanation of how to write a hook for an informational essay. He is unsure about how to create an engaging "how" question for his hook. Powerful Pencil raises his eraser. Ms. Mostly Interesting calls on him and then answers his question. Powerful Pencil asks the students, "How many of you had the same question that I did?" Out of his class of twenty students, eight students raise their hands.

Next, Successful Stapler provides a preview for the next chapter. She acts out reading, writing, and doing mathematics. The students are successful in correctly guessing her actions. "Yay! Let's learn how to be successful in reading, writing, and math!", the fourth graders shout.

Reflection Time

Powerful Pencil and Successful Stapler would like you to reflect on this chapter.

Which **two strategies from this chapter** would you like to immediately practice and **why?**

Strategy # _____
Page #   _____
Why: _____

_____

_____

_____

_____

_____

Strategy # _____
Page #   _____
Why: _____

_____

_____

_____

_____

_____

CHAPTER 5

I CAN SUCCESSFULLY READ, WRITE, AND DO MATH

A BRIEF POWERFUL STORY

The students are happily sitting in different parts of their classroom. The instrumental jazz song, "What A Wonderful World" by Louis Armstrong, is playing as fifth grade students enthusiastically read. Powerful Pencil enters the classroom with this book. He leans against a desk, since it is hard for him to sit, and begins reading this chapter. Powerful Pencil is smiling.

When it's time to turn and talk, he shares, "I am learning how to become a successful and joyful reader and writer." His partner, Successful Stapler says, "I can't wait to read about how to become a better writer. I need some useful writing strategies." The music stops, indicating independent reading time is over.

SNEAK PREVIEW OF STRATEGIES

 To prepare yourself, Powerful Pencil and Successful Stapler would like you to read and visualize each strategy.

Are any of these strategies part of your daily routine? If yes, you can underline or highlight that strategy.

63. Keep an exciting book with you throughout the day.

64. Ask your teachers, principal, assistant principal, friends, classmates, and parent(s) for book recommendations.

65. Whenever you are reading a picture book, chapter book, textbook, or an article, use an index card or bookmark as a tool for following along.

66. Whenever you closely read a fiction or nonfiction text that you are allowed to write on, make sure to annotate (underlining, highlighting, writing symbols, and writing notes on the paper).

67. Whenever you are reading and don't know the meaning of a word, use any vocabulary strategy you were taught. The context-clue technique (reading the sentence with that word, the sentence before, and the sentence after) to figure out the unknown meaning can be useful.

68. Never give up on a difficult reading, class assignment, homework, quiz, or test. Be persistent and always try your best. My father taught me that a winner never quits, and a quitter never wins.

69. Keep an ongoing idea list of interesting narrative, opinion/argumentative, and informational writing topics in the back of your writing notebook. Whenever you have an idea, you can write it down.

70. Whenever you are given a writing task, you can ask your teacher if you can draw your ideas first. Use your drawing to guide your writing.

71. Create a graphic organizer or outline before you begin a writing assignment. You can draw and/or write down your ideas on it.

72. Use a thesaurus to select synonyms (words that mean the same as another word) that are juicy and exciting to improve your writing and interest your reader.

73. Skip lines whenever you write a rough draft or double-space when typing your rough draft.

74. Whenever you proofread a completed writing assignment, read it out loud to yourself at school or at home.

75. Whenever you are proofreading your draft, make any corrections using a blue, green, or red pen. During peer editing, your partner should also use the same color.

76. Proofread any writing you do before showing it to your teacher or handing it in to be graded.

77. As you write or type your final draft, you can use a piece of paper folded in half, an index card, or a ruler to follow along the line you are copying from your rough draft.

78. After reviewing your spelling on a handwritten final draft or using spell check on the computer, make sure to double-check your final draft before handing it in.

79. Ask your teacher politely if he or she would be willing to review an almost-finished final draft of a writing assignment before you hand it in.

80. Whenever you are typing a writing assignment on a computer, tablet, or cellular phone, make sure to save the document after each new paragraph or use Google Docs, which saves automatically.

81. If math manipulatives (objects) are available in the classroom, use them to help you.

82. Show all work whenever you are solving a math problem.

STRATEGY #63

Keep an exciting book with you throughout the day.

Why: If you finish your work early and your teacher allows it, you can always read. Reading can be a magical experience.

Helpful Reminder: I highly recommend these five links for finding great books. If you need help selecting a book, share these links with your parent. Boys can read popular books for girls. Girls can read popular books for boys. Children can choose what they like to read.

Popular Books:

- <u>14 Books That 6- to 8-Year-Old Boys Say Are Must-Reads | Brightly</u>
- <u>13 Books That 9- to 12-Year-Old Boys Say Are Awesome | Brightly</u>
- <u>Books for Smart, Confident, and Courageous Girls | A Mighty Girl</u>
- <u>Growing Reader (Ages 6, 7, 8) | Brightly</u>
- <u>Tween (Ages 9, 10, 11, 12) | Brightly</u>

My Illustration

My Helpful Notes

STRATEGY #64

Ask your teachers, principal, assistant principal, friends, classmates, and parent(s) for book recommendations.

Why: You might enjoy reading those books and have fascinating conversations with your teachers, friends, classmates, and parent.

My Illustration

My Helpful Notes

STRATEGY #65

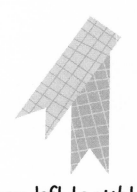

Whenever you are reading a picture book, chapter book, textbook, or an article, use an index card or bookmark as a tool for following along.

Why: It could help you pay attention to the text and keep you focused. Moving the index card or bookmark from **left to right** keeps your brain and fingers busy. It might prevent you from becoming distracted.

Helpful Reminder: If you don't have a bookmark or index card, ask your teacher for one.

<u>My Illustration</u>

My Helpful Notes

STRATEGY #66

Whenever you closely read a fiction or nonfiction text that you are allowed to write on, make sure to annotate. You can annotate by doing any or all of the following:

- o Underlining
- o Highlighting
- o Writing symbols
- o Writing notes on the margin (the side of the paper)
- o Writing questions on the margin (the side of the paper)

You can use the following annotating symbols:

√ = Agree

X = Disagree

! = Wow (surprises me)

? = Questions/wonderings

*= I want it to be included in my life.

You can ask your teacher to share other annotating symbols.

Why: You could be making connections and also might be better able to locate text evidence to answer a question or complete a task.

Helpful Reminder: If you can't write directly on the text, you can use a notebook or post-it notes.

My Illustration

My Helpful Notes

STRATEGY #67

 Whenever you are reading and don't know the meaning of a word, use any vocabulary strategy you were taught. The context-clue technique (reading the sentence with that word, the sentence before, and the sentence after) to figure out the unknown meaning can be useful.

Why: You could understand what you are reading, and it might help you get better grades.

My Illustration

My Helpful Notes

STRATEGY #68

Never give up on a difficult reading, class assignment, homework, quiz, or test. Be persistent and always try your best. My father taught me that a winner never quits, and a quitter never wins.

Why: You might be proud of yourself and confident about-facing future challenges.

Helpful Reminder: Ask for help from your teacher(s), classmates, friends, or parent.

<u>My Illustration</u>

My Helpful Notes

STRATEGY #69

Writing
Ideas

Keep an ongoing idea list of interesting narrative, opinion/argumentative, and informational writing topics in the back of your writing notebook. Whenever you have an idea, you can write it down.

Why: You could have ideas to write about and will not get stuck when you cannot come up with a writing topic. Writing can become enjoyable.

Helpful Reminder: You should request permission from your teacher before writing in the back of your notebook.

My Illustration

My Helpful Notes

STRATEGY #70

Whenever you are given a writing task, you can ask your teacher if you can draw your ideas first. Use your drawing to guide your writing.

Why: You might be a visual learner. The opportunity to draw first provides you with a plan to use when writing. It can support visual learners and/or reluctant (slow to get started) writers with producing detailed writing (Fletcher 2006).

My Illustration

My Helpful Notes

STRATEGY #71

Create a graphic organizer or outline before you begin a writing assignment. You can draw and/or write down your ideas on it.

Why: The graphic organizer or outline can support you with including all parts of the writing assignment in the draft. It can help you earn a better grade on a writing assignment.

My Illustration

My Helpful Notes

_____

_____

_____

_____

_____

_____

_____

_____

_____

_____

_____

_____

_____

STRATEGY #72

Use a thesaurus to select synonyms (words that mean the same as another word) that are juicy and exciting to improve your writing and interest your reader.

Why: Your choice of vocabulary could become stronger. As a result, your writing might be fascinating to your reader.

Helpful Reminder: You should not use a word if you don't know what it means.

My Illustration

My Helpful Notes

STRATEGY #73

Skip lines whenever you write a rough draft or double-space when typing your rough draft.

Why: You should be able to notice any edits that must be included in your final draft. It might be easier for your teacher to provide feedback on your draft. There will be space for you to make corrections. Peer editing could be easier to do.

My Illustration

My Helpful Notes

STRATEGY #74

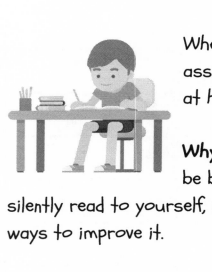

Whenever you proofread a completed writing assignment, read it out loud to yourself at school or at home.

Why: As you read each sentence out loud, you might be better able to notice any necessary edits. When you silently read to yourself, it is more difficult to identify mistakes and/or ways to improve it.

Helpful Reminder: You can request permission to move to a quiet and semi-private place in your classroom to read your writing out loud.

My Illustration

My Helpful Notes

STRATEGY #75

Whenever you are proofreading your draft, make any corrections using a blue, green, or red pen. During peer editing, your partner should also use the same color.

Why: Since these three colors are noticeable, you are more likely to include those revisions and edits in your final draft. Revisions and edits done in pencil or black pen are often hard to see.

Helpful Reminder: Ask permission from your teacher or parent before using different colored pens.

<u>My Illustration</u>

My Helpful Notes

STRATEGY #76

Proofread any writing you do before showing it to your teacher or handing it in to be graded.

Why: As a result of proofreading your writing, there should be fewer mistakes, and you could receive a better grade.

Helpful Reminder: Don't show or turn in any writing that is not your best work.

o Did I proofread my writing before showing it to my teacher?

My Illustration

My Helpful Notes

STRATEGY #77

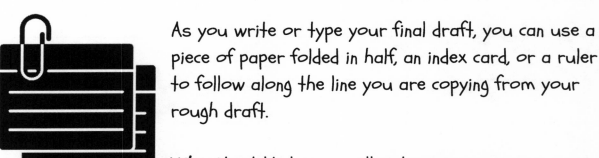

As you write or type your final draft, you can use a piece of paper folded in half, an index card, or a ruler to follow along the line you are copying from your rough draft.

Why: Most likely, you will not miss any revisions or edits; therefore, you could produce a stronger final draft.

My Illustration

My Helpful Notes

STRATEGY #78

After reviewing your spelling on a handwritten final draft or using spell check on the computer, make sure to double-check your final draft before handing it in.

Why: If you write a word that is spelled correctly but that is different from the word you planned to write, spell check will not catch it. For example, you might write the word *there*, but you had planned to write *their*.

Helpful Reminder: After you double-check your document for any spelling errors, ask an adult to proofread your work for correct spelling.

My Illustration

My Helpful Notes

STRATEGY #79

Ask your teacher politely if he or she would be willing to review an almost-finished final draft of a writing assignment before you hand it in.

Why: Requesting feedback to improve a draft before the due date could help you receive a better grade on your final draft. You will also become a better writer.

My Illustration

My Helpful Notes

_____

_____

_____

_____

_____

_____

_____

_____

_____

_____

_____

_____

_____

_____

_____

STRATEGY #80

Whenever you are typing a writing assignment on a computer, tablet, or cellular phone, make sure to save the document after each new paragraph or use Google Docs, which saves automatically.

Why: You do not want to lose any of your writing and must begin again.

Helpful Reminder: Choose a name for the saved file that you can easily remember.

My Illustration

My Helpful Notes

STRATEGY #81

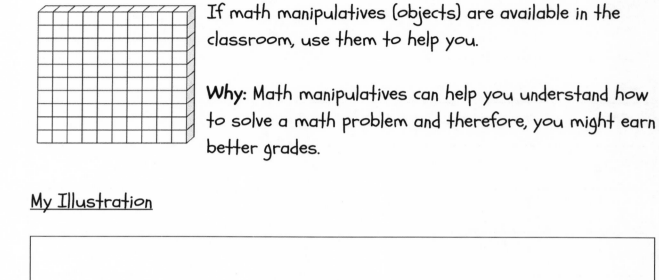

If math manipulatives (objects) are available in the classroom, use them to help you.

Why: Math manipulatives can help you understand how to solve a math problem and therefore, you might earn better grades.

My Illustration

My Helpful Notes

STRATEGY #82

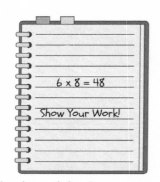

It is better not to bring fidget spinners, toys, or electronics to school, unless your teacher requests it. They can be a distraction to the classroom community.

Why: The fidget spinners, toys and/or electronics could get lost, stolen, or taken away by the teacher. You need to be able to concentrate in your classroom and complete your work.

<u>My Illustration</u>

My Helpful Notes

A SHORT SUCCESSFUL STORY

Mr. Brainstorm, the teacher, taps his chime and his students know it is time to share. Powerful Pencil happily says, "I proofread my writing out loud today for the first time. I noticed that my introduction needed some exciting synonyms and that I left out a few words."

Mr. Brainstorm says, "I'm glad that you tried out the strategy." Successful Stapler and all of the students gave Powerful Pencil a silent cheer. It was almost the end of a successful and lively day. The students are excited to have a second recess on this sunny afternoon.

Tomorrow, they will learn strategies to support them in being prepared for the next school day.

Reflection Time

Powerful Pencil and Successful Stapler would like you to reflect on this chapter.

Which **two strategies from this chapter** would you like to immediately practice and **why?**

Strategy # _____
Page # _____
Why: _____
_____
_____
_____
_____
_____

Strategy # _____
Page # _____
Why: _____
_____
_____
_____
_____
_____

CHAPTER 6

I CAN SUCCESSFULLY BE PREPARED FOR THE NEXT SCHOOL DAY

A BRIEF POWERFUL STORY

"Good afternoon, Almost Powerful Navigators of School Success! I hope you all had a fascinating and joyful day of learning", shouts Mr. Brainstorm. Most of the children smile, give a thumbs-up, or a silent cheer. They will be in an after-school program or at home soon.

Successful Stapler enthusiastically says, "You will have time for fun! However, you must always prepare for the next school day. You want to be at your best tomorrow." The children understood and put their thumbs up. They will begin reading the strategies later.

Powerful Pencil and Successful Stapler need to recharge for the next day. They both go home to relax and prepare.

SNEAK PREVIEW OF STRATEGIES

 To prepare yourself, Powerful Pencil and Successful Stapler would like you to read and visualize each strategy.

Are any of these strategies part of your daily routine? If yes, you can underline or highlight that strategy.

83. Post a wall calendar in your bedroom or on your refrigerator. Each day, write down weekly and monthly assignment due dates, tests, field trips, and school events on the calendar using a marker. You should review the dates on the calendar every morning, afternoon, and evening.

84. Complete your homework shortly after you arrive home or during an after-school program.

85. Complete your homework in an area that is free from distractions.

86. Take some short breaks when you are doing your homework, like going on a walk, exercising, or drinking some water.

87. As you complete a homework assignment, cross it out in your homework notebook or planner.

88. After you finish your homework, put it in your folder or binder, and then put that in your bookbag.

89. Make sure your homework is neatly done and handed in to your teacher without any wrinkles or food stains.

90. Don't make excuses for not completing your class work or homework. Make sure to get it done by the due date.

91. Keep the inside of your bookbag neat. Every day, you should clean out your bookbag. You can decide which items need to stay inside and what papers can be left at home or thrown out.

92. Have your parent sign any school notes, graded tests, graded quizzes, or trip permission slips the same day you receive them. Then immediately put them in a folder and into your bookbag.

93. Whenever you are required to bring home a school note, graded test, graded quiz, or trip permission slip to be signed by a parent, make sure your parent signs it, not you.

94. Whenever you receive your report card, read it carefully and be prepared to discuss it with your family.

95. Before you go to sleep, choose your clothes for the next school day, and put them on a chair or table.

96. Approximately fifteen minutes before you go to sleep, do a relaxing activity such as listening to music, journal writing, or reading.

97. Avoid going to sleep while you are feeling sad or angry. If anything is bothering you, speak to a friend or family member.

98. Avoid using technology (television, video games, Internet, and texting) half an hour before you go to sleep.

99. Sleep approximately nine to eleven hours each night.

100. Set your alarm clock or ask your parent to wake you up fifteen minutes earlier than your normal wake-up time.an exciting book with you throughout the day.

STRATEGY #83

Post a wall calendar in your bedroom or on your refrigerator. **Each day**, write down weekly and monthly assignment due dates, tests, field trips, and school events on the calendar using a marker. You should review the dates on the calendar every morning, afternoon, and evening.

Why: This could help you to not miss any assignment deadlines and to prepare for upcoming tests and events. You could become stronger with managing your time, which will be practical for the rest of your life, for the rest of school until you get a job.

Helpful Reminder: You could use a different colored marker for each type of item to record—assignment due dates, tests, field trips, and school events.

My Illustration

My Helpful Notes

STRATEGY #84

Complete your homework shortly after you arrive home or during an after-school program.

Why: You will be prepared for the next school day. During the rest of the afternoon and evening, you could be able to participate in other activities or just relax.

My Illustration

My Helpful Notes

STRATEGY #85

Complete your homework in an area that is free from distractions.

Why: You might be able to concentrate and accomplish your homework at a quicker speed.

My Illustration

My Helpful Notes

STRATEGY #86

Take some short breaks when you are doing your homework, like going on a walk, exercising, or drinking some water.

Why: These breaks could provide an opportunity to recharge your brain to focus.

<u>My Illustration</u>

My Helpful Notes

STRATEGY #87

As you complete a homework assignment, cross it out in your homework notebook or planner.

Why: This technique forces you to be aware of what homework assignments you have completed thus far. This action can support you with organization.

<u>My Illustration</u>

My Helpful Notes

STRATEGY #88

After you finish your homework, put it in your folder or binder, and then put that in your bookbag.

Why: You will be prepared for the next day, and you will have one less thing to do in the morning.

Helpful Reminders: After putting your homework in your bookbag, pack whatever you need **(except refrigerated items)** in your bookbag for the next day. Don't forget to put your three sharpened pencils in your bookbag.

My Illustration

My Helpful Notes

STRATEGY #89

Make sure your homework is neatly done and handed in to your teacher without any wrinkles or food stains.

Why: You might be proud of your work, and your teacher won't be disappointed. You are taking responsibility as a student.

<u>My Illustration</u>

My Helpful Notes

STRATEGY #90

Don't make excuses for not completing your class work or homework. Make sure to get it done by the due date.

Why: Your job is to do your work. You might receive a poor grade and/or get in trouble if the homework is not completed by the due date.

My Illustration

My Helpful Notes

STRATEGY #91

Keep the inside of your bookbag neat. Every day, you should clean out your bookbag. You can decide which items need to stay inside and what papers can be left at home or thrown out.

Why: You could become organized; therefore, you will lose less classwork and homework assignments. You could become stronger in time management since you won't waste time looking for missing items.

Helpful Reminders: Ask your teacher(s) what you must keep and what you can throw out.

<u>My Illustration</u>

My Helpful Notes

STRATEGY #92

Have your parent sign any school notes, graded tests, graded quizzes, or trip permission slips the same day you receive them. Then immediately put them in a folder and into your bookbag.

Why: You could feel good about yourself, and you won't get in trouble.

<u>My Illustration</u>

My Helpful Notes

STRATEGY #93

Whenever you are required to bring home a school note, graded test, graded quiz, or trip permission slip to be signed by a parent, **make sure that your parent signs it, not you.**

Why: It is best to be honest. Your parent has the right to know about your grades, behavior, and upcoming events and field trips. There is no choice in this matter.

Helpful Reminder: If you are caught signing any of these documents, you won't be trusted and will face consequences.

My Illustration

My Helpful Notes

STRATEGY #94

Whenever you receive your report card, read it carefully and be prepared to discuss it with your family.

Why: It is your job to know which subjects you are successful at and which one(s) you struggle with. You need to know why you received each grade. You must take responsibility for your learning to become a successful student. Sometimes, your grades help determine what type of middle school, high school, and college you could attend.

Helpful Reminders: Whenever you discuss your report card with a parent, it is helpful to begin with your best grade(s). If you did not do as well or poorly in any of your subjects, explain to your parent what happened and how you will improve. You can also ask your parent for help.

<u>My Illustration</u>

My Helpful Notes

STRATEGY #95

Before you go to sleep, choose your clothes for the next school day, and put them on a chair or table.

Why: It could save you time in the morning since you will have one less decision to make.

My Illustration

My Helpful Notes

_____

_____

_____

_____

_____

_____

_____

_____

_____

_____

_____

_____

_____

STRATEGY #96

Approximately fifteen minutes before you go to sleep, do a relaxing activity such as listening to music, journal writing, or reading.

Why: These activities could put you in a peaceful mood; therefore, you will sleep better.

My Illustration

My Helpful Notes

STRATEGY #97

Avoid going to sleep while you are feeling sad or angry. If anything is bothering you, speak to a friend or family member.

Why: You could be able to fall asleep more easily, avoid nightmares, and wake up in a better mood.

My Illustration

My Helpful Notes

STRATEGY #98

Avoid using technology (television, video games, Internet, and texting) half an hour before you go to sleep (Petersen 2011).

Why: The melatonin levels (which help you fall and stay asleep) in your body will not be decreased (Petersen 2011). You could be able to fall asleep more quickly and remain asleep.

<u>My Illustration</u>

My Helpful Notes

STRATEGY #99

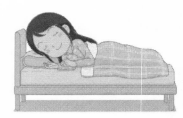

Sleep approximately nine to eleven hours each night (Petersen 2011; www.sleepforkids.org).

Why: Your body requires this quantity of daily sleep to handle all the next day's academic, emotional, and physical challenges.

<u>My Illustration</u>

My Helpful Notes

STRATEGY #100

Set your alarm clock or ask your parent to wake you up fifteen minutes earlier than your normal wake-up time.

Why: You will have extra time in the morning to prepare yourself for the day. Waking up fifteen minutes earlier could prevent you from feeling rushed.

My Illustration

My Helpful Notes

A SHORT SUCCESSFUL STORY

It's almost time for bed. The preparations are done. Powerful Pencil and Successful Stapler both listen to some jazz and write in their journals.

Forty-five minutes before they went to sleep, they both texted each other, "Good night! Sleep well. See you tomorrow."

That night, every student was thinking about one of the strategies from this chapter as they drifted off to sleep. The alarm clocks were set up to wake up the students fifteen minutes earlier than usual. Good night and pleasant dreams!

Reflection Time

Powerful Pencil and Successful Stapler would like you to reflect on this chapter.

Which **two strategies from this chapter** would you like to immediately practice and **why?**

Strategy # _____
Page # _____
Why: _____

_____

_____

_____

_____

Strategy # _____
Page # _____
Why: _____

_____

_____

_____

_____

CONCLUSION

Congratulations on transforming into a Powerful Third, Fourth, or Fifth Grade Navigator of School Success. I hope you enjoyed the handbook and found it fascinating and useful. As you continue to practice these strategies, you could become a happier, more confident, and successful student. Some days might be frustrating. It is still important to do your best every day. Thank you for taking charge of your education! You can make a positive difference in this world!

I am happy to answer your questions, listen to your feedback, and hear your ideas. You can contact me at www.toddfeltman.com and https://www.instagram.com/successfulschoolnavigator.

ACKNOWLEDGEMENTS

There have been amazing and supportive people who helped me produce and publish this interactive handbook. They all deserve a handshake, fist bump, high five, hug, and much applause. Thank you so much!

SchoolRubric Publisher: Wallace, Richard, and Robert – Your support and constructive feedback was most appreciative! I enjoyed our virtual collaborative meetings. Wallace, thank you for believing in my book idea. Your strategic layout and graphic design made this book a masterpiece. Richard, your notable editing was beneficial. It significantly helped me improve my style of writing. Robert, your genuine advice and specific compliments were helpful! The three of you helped make my "dream" of publishing this handbook a reality.

The incredible detailed illustrators from Dream Computers – I love how you designed both Powerful Pencil and Successful Stapler.

Maude Wiltshire, former colleague and friend for designing the dynamic illustrations on the handbook cover – Your talented artistic vision made Powerful Pencil and Successful Stapler a reality. Your feedback on the cover layout was most appreciated.

Tami Boyce, Illustrator – Your remarkable and practical guidance helped me out tremendously.

Fifth Grade Class 501 and their teacher from Brooklyn and Third Grade Class 208 from Manhattan – Their constructive and thoughtful feedback made this handbook more engaging and relevant.

My fantastic elementary school principal, Allan Shedlin and Incredible Elijah Lee, Youth Activist and High School Student – Your wonderful forewords made this book even better.

My family has been a source of incredible support and inspiration. I could not have published this book without each of you.

I truly want to thank **my mom, Arlene, my dad, Doug, my stepmother, Jeanne, and my brother, Alex** for supporting me with my education, career, and building my self-confidence. I love you all so much and am so proud of all you've accomplished.

Mom, you've been incredible! My handbook is published. Your vision and dedication to your successful businesses were a source of inspiration as I wrote this book. Thank you for pushing me to do my best.

As a young boy, **Dad,** I will never forget those powerful words you shared with me: *a quitter never wins, and a winner never quits.* I have carried this mantra throughout the years. Despite the obstacles, I never quit. I am thrilled I made it past Mile 20: The Wall (New York City Marathon).

Jeanne, thank you for being an effective listener and a significant member of my cheering squad.

Alex, you've been a source of inspiration. It was motivational watching you navigate and succeed in your education and social world from nursery school to adulthood.

Thank you to **Aunt Gayle, Uncle Stanley, Cousin Amy, David, Cousin Samantha, Cousin Alexandra, Aunt Dorey, Cousin Brian, Shelia, Cousin Kevin, Cousin Neal, Karen, Aunt Lee, and Claire** for your interest, support, and love.

Thank you to all the **prekindergarten, elementary-school, middle-school, undergraduate, and graduate students** who I have taught during the last twenty-five plus years. Your enthusiasm, engagement, and curiosity constantly made teaching a thrilling adventure! You always let me know when a stretching break was necessary or how important it is to laugh. You inspired me to write this handbook.

Thank you to all of **the teachers, coaches, paraprofessionals, principals, assistant principals, parent coordinators, school personnel, superintendents, and deputy superintendents** that I have professionally collaborated with. I learned so much from each of you. You increased my knowledge in building positive relationships with students and making instruction relevant. I appreciate your support in guiding students to become **Powerful Navigators of School Success**.

Craig Palmer, a spectacular mentor, lifelong friend, and camp counselor– I met you when I was an eleven-year-old camper at Kamp Kohut, a sleep away camp in Maine and fortunately, you became my bunk and soccer counselor. Our friendship has lasted for almost forty years. Your clear constructive writing feedback and kind heart is invaluable! With your bountiful support, you went beyond the call of duty. Thank you so much, **Craig**!

Fran, Wife of Craig, I appreciated your support and being an amazing listener. Our everlasting friendship is magical.

Deb Eldridge, fantastic former professor, and Dean for providing constructive feedback about my handbook.

My wonderful **friends** who encouraged and supported me. You're all the best!

REFERENCES

Fletcher, R. 2006. *Boy Writers: Reclaiming Their Voices*. Portland, ME: Stenhouse Publishers.

Park, A. 2012. "The Reason for Recess: Active Children May Do Better in School." *Time Magazine*, January 16. http://content.time.com/time/magazine/article/0,9171,2103732,00.html.

Petersen, A. 2011. "Grown-Up Problems Start at Bedtime." *Wall Street Journal*, July 18.

Sleep for Kids. (n. d.). *Teaching Kids the Importance of Sleep*. http://www.sleepforkids.org.

"U.S. Kids Not Drinking Enough Water Each Day." 2015. *HealthDay*, June 11. http://consumer.healthday.com/kids-health-information-23/child-development-news-124/u-s-kids-not-drinking-enough-water-each-day-700291.html.

ABOUT THE AUTHOR

Todd Jason Feltman, PhD, has spent over twenty-five years working in New York City Elementary and Middle Public Schools and local independent schools. He has been a classroom teacher, specialty writing teacher, mentor teacher, literacy coach, and assistant principal. Feltman is also an adjunct assistant professor in Childhood Education at Hunter College. He believes passionately that students can become powerful navigators of school success. They can take charge of their education.

Feltman has three master's degrees: one in childhood education, one in literacy education, and one in school supervision and administration. He received his doctorate in urban education from the Graduate Center at the City University of New York. His dissertation examined the gender achievement gap in reading and writing of fourth and fifth grade boys versus girls. Feltman's Bachelor of Science in Hotel Administration is from the University of New Hampshire.

ABOUT THE BOOK ILLUSTRATOR

Dream Computers, a company situated in India provides a wide range of professional digital solutions and web-based services and is the home of visionary illustrations that breathe life into your brand's story for the past 18 years! Dream Computers is a haven for those seeking exceptional, captivating, and truly unique illustrations that leave a lasting impression. https://www.dreamlogodesign.com

ABOUT THE COVER ILLUSTRATOR

Maude E. Wiltshire, Ph.D, is an art educator who teaches high school students and young adults with autism and developmental disabilities. She trains graduate student art teachers to work in the special education art classroom. She has presented on topics related to art making for non-verbal students with autism in art at education conferences nationally and around the world. Maude is a world traveler and also teaches English as a Foreign Language internationally. As an artist, Maude practices architecture, landscape, and street photography. Maude lives and works in New York City. www.maudewiltshire.com

Made in the USA
Middletown, DE
30 August 2024

59428821R00168